Revolving Love

Revolving LOVE

A'JA SIMMS

REVOLVING LOVE

iUniverse books may be ordered through booksellers or by contacting:

iUniverse
1663 Liberty Drive
Bloomington, IN 47403
www.iuniverse.com
1-800-Authors (1-800-288-4677)

ISBN: 978-1-4917-8368-9 (sc)
ISBN: 978-1-4917-8369-6 (e)

Library of Congress Control Number: 2015920844

Print information available on the last page.

iUniverse rev. date: 12/15/2015

Dedication

This book is dedicated to my son. You will forever conquer your obstacles. I love you.

Thank you to my Parents-Reginald Sr. and Rosemary and my brother Reggie, Jr.

Thank you TFMS for your support.

Acknowledgements

Thank you to the Almighty GOD for your Agape love. I am eternally grateful for the love you poured into me daily.

Thank you to my Angelic crew. I love you.

Contents

Childhood Seasons

Winter-Wood burning fireplaces with a delicious aroma of cinnamon and allspice

Spring-Honeysuckles and Roses every morning

Autumn-Fall air filled with priceless laughter coupled with the fragrance of apples and pumpkins

Summer-Humid Breeze blowing thru the air

Every room memories

Every smell a harmony

Every sound delicious to hear

Every childhood vision blood, sweat, and tears remains etched in my heart forever.

Battle of One Heart & One Mind

("I'm not supposed to hold it in" repeated throughout poem, softly)

Heart: I'm not supposed to hold it in

Mind: I'm not supposed to hold it in

Heart: Lash out!

Mind: Quiet! Hold it in.

Heart: Say something, NOW!

Mind: No don't.

Heart: They're HURTING YOU, Stop them!

Mind: Just go to sleep and wait for a new day.

Heart: Over and over again, HURT!

Mind: You use to it.

Heart: Make It STOP! WHY? WHY?

Mind: Someone has to get it.

Heart: I'm tired. I've tried!

Mind: People are busy.

Heart: Selfish, cold-hearted, no conscience

Mind: Plus, you can't blame fools and/or the unteachable

Heart: I'm not supposed to hold it in

Mind: Who will listen?

Heart: I'm not supposed to hold it in

Mind: I'm not supposed to hold it in

A'Ja Simms

?sOULmATE?

I can't begin to tell you how I felt

To know what I knew, to feel what I felt

That we belong together.

I knew it from Day 1

I knew

Spiritual.

But you had no clue

You knew you wanted someone else.

You were attracted to her body

That's pretty much it.

Physical.

Every time we talked, texted or hung out

I ached from knowing the truth

My heart just wanted to yell it out

But I didn't.

Every night I cried because no matter what I felt *you* had to figure it out for yourself

Emotional.

You had to choose who you wanted to love

Spiritual or Physical?

Now you feel what I felt …

Emotional

Mini Breakdown

I'm tired of being brave. I no longer want to put on a 'church face'. I can't stand the crying in the dark. I deserve to collapse in someone's arms and have them tell me "Let go, I got your back" I don't want to be the strongest one all the time.

When will I get my chance to be nurtured?

When is will my moment come

to let it completely go

(wiping tears)

(sigh)

Oh

I have to start cooking

time to prepare for tomorrow's schedule

don't forget to … …

I Think I See Love

How do I even tell you how you make me feel?

I like u

I want u

I can see you being mine

Omgoodness!

It's right there

Like a mist around the corner

My hands are reaching out

they're stretched wide

It's there.

No there

I'm not imaging it

I feel it

NO IT'S RIGHT THERE!!!

Why can't I grab it?

I feel like it's taking over me

Every thought of you shuts my down

All the way down

It makes me curl up like baby in a fetal position

I don't want the anxiety

I want the excitement

I feel the passion

(deep breath)

It's so overwhelming that I want you.

Star of Truth

I knew I heartbroken when I looked out a second story window into the night sky. I was trying to fight back the tears that were pouring out. I stared at a single bright star. It wasn't the beauty of the usual warm night that made me cry. It also wasn't the single bright star right in front of my eyes. My heart needs healing from an enormous amount of love lost. As I looked out the balcony I could only immediately wish and pray that my heart would be rescued by my prince charming. The fairytale of every happy-ever-after princess' dream. The prince begging for forgiveness and pleading her to receive his unconditional love. *Yeah right!* Not in a young Black woman's life. Not after all the Hell I had gone thru. By the way, I was stupid in the whole relationship. I was in love with myself. Cause he didn't love me. That's why the uncontrolled tears, now I know the complete truth. It hurts! A little time from the breakup and years of complete denial on my part.

Love in Silence

I loved you once

nor can this heart be quiet

for it would seem that love still lingers there

But don't be troubled by it any further

I would in way embarrass you,

O' my Roadrunner

I love you without hope

a mute offender

What jealous pangs

what shy despairs I knew

A love as deep as this, as true, as tender

God grant me another chance to love him again, the gift you bestowed upon me once before

A second chance I plead with you because He already blessed you with yours

I show you, U show me

I show u love; u show me evil. I'm so much more than the pornographic images u want me 2 act out.

My mouth is a key part of expressions from my heart, it's not just a tool 2 pleasure u.

My body is the vessel that my Spirit lives in, my body is not here on Earth for u 2 aggressively force yourself on me

My feelings are what makes me human, but u chose to use them against me hurt me with.

Again

I never thought I would be writing about a broken heart from you. Again! You promised you wouldn't leave. Again! This time you can't blame your job. But yet you disappeared. Again! Without an explanation. Again! I stood up for myself. I confessed the overflowing doubt in your words and overwhelming numbness from your expressions. I spoke up for once. But you left me. Again! Speechless. Again! Wandering. Again! Were the feelings of your perfect words you spoke real? Was the laughter of our shared memories real? Was your comforting hug real? Were our unrestricted kisses real? Was the dreamy attention you flooded me with real? Were you ever real, or just a second ending from a heart break healed? Again! I don't know the answers. But again, I'm left wandering what I could have done differently.

To My Baby Girl

I couldn't keep from looking at you. They're like vultures staring at me.

Look.

Don't look.

Look.

Everyone's watching.

She's beautiful. I want to hold her and never let her go. I want her to know me. I want to take her back. I see me in her face. Ever since your birth day my heart has been with you. Our bond is eternal. The ultimate gift is our reunion. I'll be patient even until Heaven.

Advantage

You said you're proud of me for not allowing people to take advantage of me

Lies

Deceit

Betrayal

Silence

Selfishness

Cache

Soul sucking

Spirit Veil

M.I.A. (missing in action)

You're the Biggest Offender!

What do I do?

My heart is calling for you. What do I do? I freaked out! I pushed you away because I'm too scared of how much I love you. Just the thought of you-your essence, your spirit, your vibe, your aura makes me shake (from fear)! You are everything I ever want to much more than I could ever dream. The whole man of God in you command me to be the whole woman of God in me. What do I do? I know what you felt. When I think of you, my mind deletes every thought, my daily agenda, how I'm supposed to function. Your love simply overwhelms me. Our love is speechless. There are no words created to describe or even explain it. People side eye us when were around. We can't blame them. We can't hide the electricity in the air when we're in the same building or the chemistry when we enter the same room. Oh gosh! What do I do?

Wedding Bands

A ring of peace.

A ring of hope.

A ring of Love.

A ring of understanding.

A ring of doubt.

A ring of trust.

A ring of Faith.

A reign of unity.

No World Without Love

Why live in this mean world if there's no love to live for

Only one thing that is a fact

You can't get into Heaven thinking like that

That's the only reason that I could think of

Since I'm living in a world without love.

Friend to Love

You won't let me go, but I can't hold not telling you that I love you. I don't know if you want to hear it. It's killing me inside if I don't let you know something. Fighting daily with the decision to tell or not to tell. How do I express to you without running you off? Do I open the flood gates or just quietly be your friend? How do I act? Kissing you passionately or just a friendly head nod. I'll risk it. Is it worth it? Possible years of intimacy destroyed. I'll be experimenting, trying to communicate that bond between us, to further explore it with you. Can we can, Can we. Do we, Do we. Is it worth me gambling with my friend for love?

Beginning Love

Falling in love with you isn't as hard as I thought. I thought that it wouldn't happen to me again. But I met you and my whole life did a 180. Why have I fallen in love with you? You should love me, but you don't. I have never given you a reason not to. I broke a promise to myself. I promised myself I wouldn't fall in love with you. You know the reasons why. But you can't predict love. I have these feelings for you and you're never around for me to express them. I can't bottle my feelings up. They're gonna still shine thru.

SOOOO Dumb ...

How could I be sooo dumb …

>To think someone as handsome as you, can love me too.

How could I be sooo dumb …

>To think that I could be the only one.

How could I be sooo dumb …

>To think you would care for me, as much as I care for you.

How could I be sooo dumb …

>To think that finally maybe I've found the One.

How could I be sooo dumb …

>To think that I could release trust in you.

How could I be sooo dumb …

>To think that I could handle the pain.

How could I've been soooo dumb.

Hunny Bunny

You're my bunny because of the way my Soul hops for you.

You're my bunny because of the warm feelings your body gives when you're lying next to me.

You're my bunny because you always make me smile just like a child in a candy store.

You're my bunny because when you're away from me, my heart flops with the weight of missing you.

You're my Hunny because of the sweet taste of your beautiful lips.

You're my Hunny because your love is warm as it flows all thru me.

You're my Hunny because your essence and presence gets better with age.

You're my Hunny because every time you passionately look at me it refreshes our relationship.

You will always be my Hunny Bunny.

Who, What, When, and How?

What did I do to deserve your faithful love?

Be yourself, that's what made me fall in love with you.

How did our relationship get so deep?

We grew together.

When will I ever stay out of the clouds?

Forever our love will always lift us high.

Who can blame us for being so happy?

No one, people only dream of this kind of happiness.

I wonder

I wonder, do you know how much I really and truly love you?

I wonder, do you know how much I would & will do anything for you?

I wonder, do you know how much I die inside at the thought of losing you?

I wonder, do you know how much my heart aches when you're away from me?

I wonder, do you know how much I think about you?

I wonder, do you know how much I dream about our future together?

I wonder, do you know how much I want you more & more, day by day?

I wonder, do you know how much I need you in my life?

I wonder, do you know how happy I've been since you came into my life?

I wonder, do you know how much creativity has shined thru me because of the passion I have for you?

I wonder, if I'm the only one, between us, that have any of these feelings.

Waiting

What if what you been waiting for never comes? What if you die still hoping for your dreams and desires to manifest? What if they don't come true? *(shrugging my shoulders)* It's not like you can sue *God*. What if you pass away does your dreams evaporate with your Spirit or are they a sweet scent lingering in the air? What if *waiting* is just a man-made illusion? Maybe it never even existed. Your clergy tells you to wait. Your family tells you to wait. The elders tell you to wait. People say it all the time, *wait!* When does waiting graduate to action?

Love

People say love comes when you are not looking. I didn't think I had to look for love. How do I look for something that I'm made from? Only type of love I see is unconditional. God said love is a *need* for us not a want. So how can I look for something that is supposed to be already here? I want just a taste of *love*. Any kind of *love*. A genuine smile or the hard to find loyal friend. I honestly want that fantasy dream of my true love. I'm starting to heal so I can open myself up to receive love. I learning to see amazing beauty in love.

Skin

Skin to skin

Your skin to my skin

Touch my skin with your finger like it's the only thing that will keep you alive

Your cool skin gently touching my warm skin

The heat from your skin

I absorb your skin

My skin, your skin

Our skin is eternally One.

Not Surprised

hate on me

Keep hating on me

The more you hate on me, the more GOD LOVES ME

That's all you got?

You can't do better than that?

Well, my *God* protects me. … comforts me … and definitely warms with *Peace*!

Close your mouth cause *God* not finished shocking you, yet!

That might not sound good and It absolutely won't feel good to you.

But the Love *God* has wipes all that negativity out like it never existed.

So *hate* on me

Come on

Come with it!

Sshhh

Now close your mouth!

Imma Be Okay

U used me but that's alright Imma be okay

U thought u could just steal my joy away.

U lied and deceived me over and over again

Until even your mind didn't know it was pretend.

U used me but that's alright Imma be okay

U absorbed every emotion while my body acted like it was under some strange love potion.

U used me but that's alright Imma be okay

U seek me for prayers while you walked the streets doing things people wouldn't dare.

U used me but that's alright Imma be okay

I finally understand that GOD's Grace flows to me each and every day.

U used me but that's alright Imma be okay

Your hustle them first mentality will get u nowhere fast

If u keep taking from others your blessings will definitely pass.

You Understood Me

You frustrate me

You're getting on my nerves

Why you keep looking at me

What?

U just sit there watching me. Your eyes following my every movement but you say nothing. You gently pull my shirt and give me the deepest kiss GOD allowed a person to give. I close my eyes and melt in your arms. When I open my eyes I see the world we created, our beautiful children. All because you understood me.

I Cried

I cried for joy and happiness.

I cried for the pain you go thru.

I cried because I think about you every second of every minute.

I cried because of the thought of losing you.

I cried because I care about you so much.

I cried because the love I have for you slays me inside.

I cried because this much love will only cause pain.

I cried because I want you in my life forever and that scares me.

I cried because I need your love to continue to inspire me.

I cried because all of these feelings and expressions came from me, not you.

I cried because I'm putting my heart on the line, only to be crushed again.

I cried because I thought you loved me too.

I cried because I prayed for this to true.

It's Not a Toy

You played with my emotions

You *played* with my emotions

You played *with* my emotions

You played with *my* emotions

You played with my *emotions*

I'm not your damn toy. Pushing my buttons for your psychotic satisfaction. You get off on the thrill, you get high off my broken heart.

YOU played with my emotions

You PLAYED with my emotions

You played WITH my emotions

You played with MY emotions

You played with my EMOTIONS

You mastered the game expertly

Level 1 Disrespect

Level 2 Dishonesty

Level 3 Discouraging

Level 4 Dismissal

My emotions got played by you

Beep, beep GAME OVER!

Been Thru

It sickens me sometimes reading what I've been going thru. The only release is reading "been" thru, which represents past. That equals not going thru that particular pain right now. I've been thru which means I came from and that equals life lessons learned. I'm going thru which means I'm coming out of and that will equal the trial is in the past

Going thru

Get thru

Forgiving In

Been thru

Healing Forward

Pray

Pray, pray, pray for the Holy Spirit today

Pray, pray, pray the danger away

Pray, pray, pray for comfort and peace

Pray, pray, pray for evil to cease

Pray, pray, pray for your heart to be healed

Pray, pray, pray your Spirit and Soul, satan won't steal.

Strong

Be a precious stone, stand alone

You should never have to defend your honor

But always demand respect

You should never become a prisoner

But remain a solitaire warrior

Broken Family

Broken family with jagged edge pieces. Sharp unamendable fragments floating in love. Their hearts cry and bleeds in their soul. Spirit yelling betrayals in other dimensions

Your way over there

I'm way over here

Unfair premature judgment that stands on quicksand support. Boldly walk alone with no acceptance of family. Straying black sheep from that immaculate herd. Never present, never there, different times. Secrets cutting blood ties and spreading soulful bonds. Love them from a distance to shield one's own heart

Lovers Convo#1

Lover 1: I love you more than the sun when it kisses the ocean every night.

Lover 2: I love you so much, your day can't wrong.

Lover 1: I love you so much, I can't let you go!

Lover 2: I love so much the atmosphere shifts just for us.

Lover 1: I love you more than a 10pt earthquake shaking a city.

Lover 2: I love you more than the clouds parting the way for the sun.

Lover 1: I love you more than Beverly Hills needs Botox.

Lover 2: I love you so much the other side of the world can feel it.

Lover 1: I love you more than New York needs another trash island.

Lover 2: I love you more than the deepest point of the largest ocean.

Lover 1: I love you more than you needing to wear your glasses every day.

Lover 2: I love you more than the Unites States of America deficit.

Lover 1: I love you more than the amount of times I can make you climax.

Lover 2: Damn you really do love me.

Lovers Convo #2

Lover 1: I love you more than every cell in your body

Lover 2: I love you more than every Texas house needing air conditioning.

Lover 1: I love you more than there are jobs for people.

Lover 2: I love you more than dogs panting for water.

Lover 1: I love you more than the public enjoys reality T.V.

Lover 2: I love you more than words on paper.

Lover 1: I love you more than an artist needing a muse.

Lover 2: I love you more than my Spirit need a body.

Lover 1: I love you more than people needing to stay out of my business.

Lover 2: I love you more than gossip likes to spread.

Lover 1: I love you more than the ceases in your hand.

Lover 2: I love you more than the veins in my body that carry warm blood to and from my heart.

Lover 1: I love you more than the amount of time it takes to break a steel wall.

Lover 2: I love you more than unblocking (warming) a cold heart.

Lovers Convo #3

Lover 1: I love you more than a crushed Spirit could cry.

Lover 2: I love you more than the combination of salty and sweet.

Lover 1: I love you more than my physical breath could inhale.

Lover 2: I love you more than dry hair needs oil.

Lover 1: I love you more than vitamins nourishing your body.

Lover 2: I love you more than the dust particles that float in your house.

Lover 1: I love you more than you care to know.

Lover 2: I love you more than your heart will allow you to give.

Lover 1: I love you more than the boundaries of *respect*.

Lover 2: I love you more than the *truth*.

U don't

U don't have to love me

U don't have to care about me

U don't have to want me

U don't have to listen to me

U don't have to hear me

U don't have to touch me

U don't have to hold me

U don't have to understand me

U don't have to think about me

U don't have to remember me

U don't have to love me

I can't make U!

Love Bye

Every time you get me into trouble

My mind gets cloudy

My heart beats fast.

I make stupid decisions and dumb demands

I get hurt. *Constantly*

leave, Leave, LEAVE ME ALONE

We don't get along

You're supposed to be a gift

Love you're representing yourself as a curse

bye, BYE, keep walking by

You Ain't No Good

Just like all the rest. You lie, cheat, and steal. Lies you have told so often that they become true-in your mind. Cheat so much that you believe your own lies. Stealing my love, throwing it away like trash. You cheated me by not loving me back. Lied so much I thought I was the crazy one. You think you're the best Creator made. You stole your future away. You're just like all the rest. Probably no good

I Know You Don't

I know you don't care. My hurt, my pain, my love, my heart. I know you don't care. It's easy for you to disappear. I know you don't care. Because your actions lie on your words. I know you don't care. Even now my heart breaking by the second. I know you don't care. And I still want the best for you. I know you don't care. Because if you did there would be tears of joy not of sorrow. I know you don't care. Check it you wouldn't reading this right now.

The Silence

The Silence of the relationship ending

The dead air of no communication

The silence of loneliness setting in.

It's silent.

LOVE

Love is all hype that doesn't exist

Love is weak ass emotion

Love is me compromising

Love is your endless lies

Love is me forgiving you-moving forward

Love is your pranks and jokes

Love is how I express my feelings

Love is you being shady

Love is my support and spiritual guidance

Love is your nosey and mischievous actions

Love is how open my communication was

Love is your empty promises

Love is me becoming your instant babysitter in public

Love is your immature idea for fun

Love is answering the phone after you destroyed our night out

Love is you having selective amnesia

Love is how I want the best for you

Love is you taking me for granted

Love is quality time with you

Love is always needing a group to accompany you

Love is a lot of things positive

Sometimes love gets displayed negativity.

Releasing Baggage

I haven't felt this good in months, in years. Didn't imagine love would find me again. But if this is what it feels like I don't want it. He's gone. I had to leave him alone. Emotionless. Every blue moon he showed life. His actions didn't show love. Who are you saving face for? If you're in love, who are you trying to impress? Not me. I'm not impressed. I'm disappointed. I'm hurting? HEARTBROKEN! You don't even have the emotions to care. It's a game to you. *Spotlight, Limelight!* All eyes on you. Your friends have to try to convince me because you have tons of layers. I can't possibly peel them. They need to be ripped off instantly like a soiled bandage. I peel you replace the layers back on. Shady, close in! I have to live my life too. Who has that kind of time? You *completely* drained me!

To Reminisce or Not to Reminisce

Brokenhearted or being lonely the difference is too big to measure

I thought I was at peace

I *still smell you*, my mind wanders

Oh my gosh, my mind is wandering

I can't control it

It's your scent

It's on my shirt

Yeah, hours ago you held me that tight

Maybe I inhaled you thru my skin

The glow you gave me is pouring out in the air

no, No, NO. I gotta let go!

My Soul is done crying over you but my eyes are still tearing up

I gotta wipe them away

If I don't every tear that drops means I still love you

You're not real, you're a lie

You lied to me continually

You might as well say I was in love with myself

Why I say that?

Huh, because our foundation was built on your lies

It was those lies, those lies, his lies

So get over it already

You can't deal.

Free Yourself

Free yourself from hurt and pain

Peace enter me and fill me up until it overflows

Consume me until I am completely intoxicated

I welcome you-*peace* to disinfect my deep wounds

I overdosed on what I thought was love

I need to be FREE!

Detox me. I need *peace*.

I'll die with *Love* in me.

Love or Lust Revealed

Lust unmasked itself and revealed to me the lies

Lust showed me love, as its face.

Until I command it to be true. Show your true self *Love*!

Huh, that's what I thought.

love is a disguise

I say, reveal yourself! In the beginning I knew it was *you*

Lust, I wouldn't have given you the time of day.

So long

leave me be

I hate the sight of you

Your game I won't play.

Leave me be, be gone I command you

You're not worthy to reside in me again.

Blame Me for Love

Blame yourself, not others

Look at your involvement.

You allowed it to happen.

You opened yourself up to get hurt.

You ignored your better judgments.

You wanted something so badly you settled for something much less.

You believed the deception and accepted the disrespect.

WOW!

Was it really worth it

NOPE

I Want

I want you in my life and in my world.

I want you in my space and inside of me.

I want you on my mind, fully blocking my thoughts.

I want you to always crave me and obsess for me.

I want to gently touch your lips with mine. Brushing them so tenderly.

I want to nestle in your arms while I lay my head on your chest.

I want to hear your heart pumps rhythmically as it beats my name.

I want to drift off to sleep know that I'm protected with you.

Love Returned

Today is your day to receive the love that you poured out to me back to you. Your open expression of love has totally destroyed my protective wall. That tough wall that took years of hurt to build its solid foundation. Never a day do I want you to wake not knowing that I love and how I appreciate you. I don't want to be a taker or just a receiver. But I humbly want to be a giver a contributor to our love. I commit to filling you with the purest love. A love that never fails, a love that keeps you on the highest cloud. A love that danger and negativity can't even tough. I want you to be filled with my love that helps you to know the real me. I hope you will receive my gift of love, because excited to receive your love every day.

God Is Between Us

I asked my angels to thank your angels for guiding us to happiness. God was our light thru storms and pain. *He* still shines bright to pave this new journey. If it wasn't for *Him* the electricity I feel with you wouldn't exist. When love had to detour me, God's agape love put hope back on course. God's grace freed us to experience these new things to come. I am filled by the blessings we will share together forever.

Sweet Wish

I wish our heart didn't hurt like Fireballs.

I wish your kisses weren't as sweet as gummy bears.

I wish your body wasn't as sculpted as peanut brittle.

I wish you didn't walk around with that King Size Milky Way between your legs.

I wish your skin wasn't as silky smooth like a Godiva Bar.

Call On Love

Why would I call on *you* now?

Have you ever listened

I use to call on you a lot

Every freaking day

I lived for you

I breathe you in

What the hell you do?

Make me go thru

I didn't know how else to think

But to think about you

Every minute

Every second

You

Now

You want me to give you your millionth chance

Call on Love

And watch our eyes dance

Call on Love

Yeah I'll call on you

LOVE

I'm here!!!

WHERE ARE YOU?

Love Has a Dark Side

No one ever talks about the dark side of Love.

Like wandering why, you still alone

Eye sight gets blind as a bat

Jeopardizing your principles and morals

Making them turn into possible and might

Brain forgets that you have your own brilliant ideas

Shutting your feelings down to save energy

Because their feelings are overriding yours.

I just Can't Keep Loving You

I just can't keep loving you

thinking about you every minute

hoping you will want me

swindling myself

wandering about our future

allowing you into my life

being heartbroken time and time again

having my promises not fulfilled

letting disappointments from you become a passionate hate

you tried to stop my God given destiny and my purpose

accepting your excuses

that really are lies that destroy

releasing benefits of me to you while you abandon me

with no acknowledgement

standing by you

let me go again and again

being foolish for you

When you keep choosing her over me.

Missing Him

I miss him. I gotta stop thinking about him. That's the hardest part. I feel his energy all around me. My heart is pounding just like when he's in front of me.

My heart (my hands cover my heart)

My heart

Someone please tell my heart. Tell it, yell at it. Be aggressive with it. Scold it, demand it to heal, to move on

To let him go

If I ever thought Love could do no harm.

the *intensity*

I … can't … breath

The air is sooo thick with Love for him.

Breath deep …

Breath slow …

Exhale every pain, every ache

(SMH) I miss him

I've Been

It makes me angry that our love breaks my focus on hope. So I question it. Does my passion of love for you out weight the passion of hate for you?

I've been your safety net

your ride~or~die chick

your adventurous lover

your prayer warrior

your encourager

your listening ear

your pawn when someone pissed you off

What do I get (humph)?

You married another

Convenient.

Did I ever have value to you?

Y R U Hiding?

I'm in Love.

I had love … barely …

I called on God by crying out loud. I'm ready to Love! U made me Love. U created me to Love. I need Love 2 breath, 2 survive, 2 bless others with the overflow U rained on me. Drought, severe drought. Y am I not getting nourishment. My skin color is darkened. It dying. It's not pumping thru my veins. My bones R brittle because I lacking in it. Y R U hiding from me. I did U no harm ever, but U failed 2 protect me. I shared U with friends, family and strangers but U disappeared without an explanation. Leaving me abandoned, lonely, not understanding my true value. But God healed me so I can receive U better. Maybe U didn't get the memo. So I'll B brave & say it out loud from the top of my head 2 the tip of my toes. My Spirit calls out I NEED LOVE!

Mad Enough To Leave You

Are you serious?

you think that what

you did was okay

what you did was so out there

it just flew right over my head

Yeah, the best it did for you

was allowing me to let you go.

I should've done that a while ago.

you definitely pulled that game from the underworld

Heavenly love was nowhere around

those shanagains.

self-centeredness.

effortless.

Now go be by yourself.

Let Go

I have to let go. No matter how I feel. Flutters of my eyes sting with warm tears streaming down my face.

I gotta let go. Even my heart started to ache. Dabs of quick pricks as each beat was released.

I'm not ready to let go. I'm just not ready. I tired, really tried to prepare myself. I love you so much. I just couldn't reason with my heart.

Now I'm lost & hurt. Because you let go.

He's my ... I'm His ...

He's my sweet romance. I'm his sexy spice. Thinking of him fills me with warmth all over. I give him that youth. Hmmm that get up & go. His OOOHHH! To my BAM! I'm that mysterious flavor he craves. He's that forbidden season I haven't conquered yet. He's growls continually gives me shivers.

ssshhhh

His words go straight to my Spirit with such powerful force. The way I love on him so freely is sooo effortless. I know he's attached to "my soul" but is it enough to be worthy to call me his "mate"? To be in the room with us, embrace the atmosphere shift. They can't recognize what that unexplained energy is

Full saturation of unbreakable LOVE.

But I Can't Syndrome

I wish I could be what you need

but I can't.

I wish I could remember to call

but I can't.

I wish I could think about you all day

but I can't.

I wish I could spend quality time with you

but I can't.

I wish I could fulfill promises I made to you

but I can't.

I wish I could understand you

but I can't.

I wish I could put my pride aside

but I can't.

I wish I could be free to express myself like you.

but I can't.

I wish I could have my cake and eat it too.

but I can't.

A'Ja Simms

I Ain't Her

You can't say you love me and try to change me. You instruct me how to please you but all along it's her characteristic not mine. Understand me. Don't change me. Accept me. Don't chain me. You dismiss the best part of me. Just me being me. I don't want to be her. I want to be me. Tough decision. Think about it. I ain't her. PEACE.

Revolving Love

If I could, my arms of love would draw out every hurt you ever went thru I would tear my Spirit in half to restore yours. As childish as it may seem, I just constantly keep daydreaming about the world revolving around us. Time stands still. Our only life still. The only life still moving are us. We are one.

Protect Us

Granny, Grandpop, Parents, Brothers, Sisters, Aunts, Uncles, Cousins, Friends

please Guardian Angels protect us every day

falls, car accidents, wrong places at the wrong time, diseases took you away

please Guardian Angels protect us every day

addiction, bad relationships, poor decision were also at play

please Guardian Angels protect us every day

butterflies, blue birds, rainbows you send to us

please Guardian Angels protect us every day

weddings, childbirth, new homes you bring us

please Guardian Angels protect us every day

warm hugs and glowing love we miss from you often

You visit from Heaven

Our Guardian Angels protect us every day.

Printed in the United States
By Bookmasters